Characters
OF THE
Passion

Other Liguori/Triumph Titles by Fulton J. Sheen:

From the Angel's Blackboard

Jesus, Son of Mary

Lift Up Your Heart

Peace of Soul

Simple Truths

The Cross and the Beatitudes

Characters
OF THE
Passion

LESSONS

on

FAITH

and

TRUST

❀

FULTON J. SHEEN

✠ LIGUORI/TRIUMPH
LIGUORI, MISSOURI

Published by Liguori/Triumph
An Imprint of Liguori Publications
Liguori, Missouri
http://www.liguori.org

Nihil Obstat:
John M. A. Fearns, S.T.D.
Censor Librorum

Imprimatur:
+Francis Cardinal Spellman
Archbishop of New York

Library of Congress Cataloging-in-Publication Data

Sheen, Fulton J. (Fulton John), 1895–1979
   Characters of the passion : lessons on faith and trust / Fulton J. Sheen.
      p. cm.
   Originally published: New York : P.J. Kenedy & Sons, 1947.
   ISBN 0-7648-0229-1 (pbk.)
   1. Jesus Christ—Passion. 2. Bible. N.T. Gospels—Biography. I. Title
BT430.S47   1998
232.96—dc21   98-3175

Printed in the United States of America
02 01   5 4 3

Originally published in 1947 by P.J. Kenedy & Sons. This edition published by special arrangement with the Estate of Fulton J. Sheen.

Dedicated to
MARY IMMACULATE,
Gracious Mother
of
Divine Grace,
in Token
of
Love and Gratitude

Contents

There is no unbelief;
Whoever plants a seed beneath the sod
And waits to see it push away the clod,
He trusts in God.

Whoever says when clouds are in the sky,
Be patient, heart, light breaketh by and by,
Trusts the Most High.

Whoever sees neath the field of winter snow,
The silent harvest of the future grow
God's power must know.

—EDWARD BULWER-LYTTON

CHAPTER ONE

❀

Peter:
A Lesson on
Falling and Rising

The most interesting drama in all the world is the drama of the human soul. Were it not endowed with freedom, it might go out to war and enterprise alone and unheeded; but master of its choice, unlike the sun and stones, it can use time and things to decide its destiny, its eternity, and its judgment. Though there are many phases to these dramas, perhaps the most interesting of them all is the psychology of a fall and resurrection.

More concretely, how do some souls lose their faith, and by what steps do they later on recover it? The answer to such questions is to be found in the story of the apostle Peter, whose name appears first in the gospel narrative, and who might appropriately be called "The Fisherman Philosopher," for he asked Divine Wisdom more questions than any other of His followers. For example, "To whom shall we go?" "Where are you going?" "Why cannot I follow you?" "What shall this man do?"

To this searching intellectualist of Galilee, who was born Simon and whose name was changed to Peter, and who from the bitterness of his spirit cried out, "Depart from me, O Lord, for I am a sinful man," we go to study the steps by which he fell and the stages by which he returned. There seem to have been five stages in Peter's fall.

1. Neglect of prayer
2. Substitution of action for prayer
3. Lukewarmness
4. The satisfaction of material wants, feelings, and emotions.
5. Human respect

Neglect of Prayer. No soul ever fell away from God without giving up prayer. Prayer is that which establishes contact with Divine Power and opens the invisible resources of heaven. However dark the way, when we pray, temptation can never master us. The first step downward in the average soul is the giving up of the practice of prayer, the breaking of the circuit with divinity, and the proclamation of one's own self-sufficiency.

The night that Our Blessed Lord went out under the light of a full moon into the Garden of Gethsemani to crimson the olive roots with His own blood for our redemption, He turned to His disciples and said, "Watch and pray that you may not undergo the test. The spirit is willing, but the flesh is weak" (Matthew 26:41). Withdrawing from these three disciples about as far as a man could throw a stone—how significant a way to measure distance the night one goes to death—He prayed to His Heavenly Father, "My Father, if it is possible, let this cup pass from me; yet, not as I will, but as you will" (Matthew 26:39).

When Our Blessed Lord came back the last time to visit His disciples, He found them asleep. A woman will watch not one hour or one night, but, rather, day after day and night after night in the presence of a peril threatening her child. These men slept. If they could sleep on such an occasion, it was due to the fact that they had no adequate conception of the crisis through which Our Savior was passing, no consciousness of the tragedy that was already upon them. Finding them asleep, Our Blessed Lord spoke to Peter and said, "…What? Could you not watch one hour with me?" (Matthew 26:40). Peter had given up both watching and praying.

The Substitution of Action for Prayer. Most souls still feeling the necessity of doing something for God and the

Church turn to the solace of activity. Instead of going from prayer to action, they neglect the prayer and become busy about many things. It is so easy to think we are doing God's work when we are only in motion or being fussy.

Peter is no exception. In the turmoil of the arrest of Our Blessed Lord which followed, Peter, who had already been armed with two swords, allows his usual impetuosity to get the better of him. Slashing out rather recklessly at the armed gang, what he strikes is not a soldier at all, but a slave of the High Priest. As a swordsman Peter was a good fisherman. The slave steps aside, and the blow aimed at the crown of his head merely cuts off his ear. Our Blessed Lord restored the ear by a miracle, and then turning to Peter said, "…Put your sword back into its sheath, for all who take the sword will perish by the sword" (Matthew 26:52). Divinity has no need of it. He could summon twelve legions of angels to His aid if He wished. The Church must never fight with the weapons of the world.

The Father had offered the Son the cup, and no one could hinder His drinking it. But Peter, giving up the habit of prayer, substituted violence toward others, and all tact was lost as devotion to a cause became zeal without knowledge. Far better it would be to take a few hours from active life and spend it in communion with God, than to be busy about many things while neglecting the one thing that is necessary for peace and happiness. No such activity is a substitute for watching and praying an hour.

Lukewarmness. Experience soon proves that religious activity without prayer soon degenerates into indifference. At this stage souls become indifferent. They believe one can be too religious, too zealous, or "spend too much time in church." Peter exemplifies this truth.

A few hours later, Our Blessed Lord is led before His judges—and one is almost inclined to say, "May God forgive us for calling them judges." As that sad procession moves on in the unutterable loneliness where the God-man freely subjects Himself to the evil darts of others, the gospel records, "And Peter followed Him from afar." He had given up prayer, then action, and now he keeps his distance. Only his eyes remain on the Master.

How quickly the insincerity of action without prayer proves itself! He who was brave enough to draw a sword a few hours before now strays on behind. Christ, who once was the dominating passion of our life, now becomes incidental in religion.

We still linger as from force of habit—or perhaps even from remorse of conscience—in the footsteps of the Master, but out of the range of both His eyes and His voice. It is in such moments that souls say, "God has forgotten me," when the truth is that it is not God who leaves us, it is we who stray on behind.

Satisfaction of Material Wants, Feelings, and Emotions. Once the divine fades in life, the material begins to assert itself. The excessive dedication to luxury and refinement is always an indication of the inner poverty of the spirit. When the treasure is within, there is no need of those outer treasures that rust consumes, moths eat, and thieves break through and steal. When the inner beauty is gone, we need luxuries to clothe our nakedness.

It is only natural, therefore, to find that in the next stage of his decline, Peter should be satisfying his body. He does not go into the courtroom. He remains outside with the servants; and in the expressive language of sacred Scripture, "...when they had kindled a fire in the midst of the hall, and were sitting about it, Peter was in the midst of them" (Luke 22:55).

There is a process going on in Peter, but it is hardly progress, for it is a downward movement—walking, standing, sitting. That is exactly what Peter did. *Walking:* "He followed Him from afar." *Standing:* He went into the court and stood among the people. *Sitting:* He sat by the fire that the enemies of Christ had built. Luxury had replaced fidelity. Never before was anyone so cold before a fire!

Human Respect. The last stage in the fall is human respect, when we deny our faith or are ashamed of it under ridicule or scorn. A worldly religion will get on well with the world, but not a divine one. As Our Lord warned, "When they persecute you in one town, flee to another. Amen, I say to you, you will not finish the towns of Israel before the Son of Man comes" (Matthew 10:23).

As the blaze of that fire lighted up the face of Peter, it was possible for bystanders and those who came into the court to see his face. At that very moment when Our Blessed Lord in court was taking an oath proclaiming His divinity, Peter was taking an oath, too—not to reaffirm that Christ was the Son of the Living God, but rather to deny it.

There was the clamor of officers and the saucy laughter of a servant maid, who said, "This man too was with Jesus of Nazareth." Peter denied it. Then, another maidservant said that he was one of them, but he denied it again, saying, "...Woman, I do not know him" (Luke 22:57). Perhaps an hour passed, and then one of the men said to him, "...Surely you are one of them; for you are also a Galilean" (Mark 14:70). "...even your speech gives you away" (Matthew 26:73). Peter became angry at their repeated affirmations, and with an atavistic throwback to his fisherman days when his nets became tangled in Galilean waters, he cursed and swore again, saying, "...I do not know this man about whom you are talking" (Mark 14:71).

Human respect had gotten the better of Peter. How often others know what we ought to do, even when we have forgotten. How touchy are those consciences that have abandoned their God! How sensitive they are to even the memory that they once had the faith! Many a time I have heard such souls say, "Do not talk about it! I want to forget it." But we can never forget—even our speech betrays that we had been with the Galilean.

So if these are the steps away from the faith, what are the steps back to its embrace? They are:

1. Disillusionment
2. Response to grace
3. Amendment
4. Sorrow

Disillusionment. Since pride is a capital sin, it follows that a first condition of conversion is humility: The ego must decrease, God must increase. This humiliation most often comes by a profound realization that sin does not pay, that it never keeps its promises, that just as a violation of the laws of health produces sickness, so a violation of the laws of God produces unhappiness.

This is signified in Peter's case by the fulfillment of a prophecy made by Our Lord to Peter the night of the Last Supper. Having warned His apostles that they would be scandalized in Him that night, Peter boasted, "I will lay down my life for you" (John 13:37). And Our Lord answered, "...Will you lay down your life for me? Amen, amen, I say to you, the cock will not crow before you deny me three times" (John 13:38).

A few hours later, at the very moment that Peter cursed and swore that he knew not Christ, there came through the halls of the outer chambers of Caiaphas' court, the clear and unmistakable crowing of a cock. *Even nature is on God's side.* We may abuse it in our sins, but in the end it will abuse us. How right was Thompson when he characterized nature as having a "traitorous trueness, a loyal deceit; in fickleness to me, in loyalty to Him."

The crowing of the cock was such a childish thing. But God can use the most insignificant things in the world as the channel of His grace: the vow of a child, a word over the radio, the song of a sparrow. He will even press into the business of conversation the crowing of a cock in the dawning of the morning. A soul can come to God by a series of disgusts.

Response to Grace. The next step in the return to God after the awakening of conscience through the disillusionment of sin is on God's part. As soon as we empty ourselves, or are disillusioned, He comes to fill the void. "...No one comes to the Father except through me" (John 14:6). And Saint Luke tells us, "And the Lord turning looked on Peter" (Luke 22:61).

As sin is an aversion to God, grace is the conversion to God. Our Lord does not say, "I told you, you would fall." He does not desert us though we desert Him. He turns, once we know we are sinners. God never gives us up. The very word used here to describe the look of Our Lord is the same word used the first time Our Lord met Peter—the meaning being that "He looked through" Peter. Peter is recalled to the sweet beginnings of His grace and vocation. Judas received the lips to recall him to fellowship. Peter received a look with eyes that see us, not as our neighbors see us, not as we see ourselves, but as we really are. They were the eyes of a wounded friend, the look of a wounded Christ. The language of those eyes we shall never understand.

Amendment. As sin begins with the abandonment of mortification, so conversion implies return to it. The king in *Hamlet* asked, "Can one be forgiven and retain the offense?" There are such things as occasions of sin, namely, those persons, places, and circumstances that dry rot the soul.

Peter's conversion would not be complete unless he left that arena where maidservants, slaves, and human respect combined to make him deny the Master. No longer will he warm himself by fires, nor sit passively while his Judge is judged. The Scripture records his amendment or purgation in the simple words, "And *going forth.*" All the trappings of sin, the ill-gotten goods, the human respect he won, all these are now trampled underfoot, as "he goes out."

Sorrow. But this leaving of the tabernacles of sin would not be enough were there not sorrow. Some leave sin only because they find it disgusting. There is no real conversion until that sin is related to an offense against the Person of God. "Against Thee have I sinned," says Scripture, not against "Space-time," or the "Cosmic Universe," or the "Powers Beyond." Have a sorrow that regrets offending God because He is all good and deserving of all our love, and you have salvation.

Fittingly, therefore, do the evangelists write, "And Peter going out, wept bitterly" (Luke 22:62). His heart was broken into a thousand pieces, and his eyes that looked into the eyes of Christ, now turn into fountains. Moses struck a rock, and water came forth. Christ looked on a rock, and tears came forth. Tradition has it that Peter wept so much for his sins that his cheeks were furrowed with their penitential streams.

Upon those tears the face of the Light of the World rises, and through them comes the rainbow of hope, assuring all souls that never again will a heart be destroyed by flood of sin so long as it turns to Him Who is the Ark of Salvation, the Love of the Universe.

This closes the story of the most human of humans in the gospels, who one moment is on the top of a wave walking the sea and the next moment beneath it drowning and shrieking, "Lord, save me." One instant he says he will die with Our Lord; an hour later he denies that he knows the One for whom he would die.

Who is there who has not within himself or herself felt those same conflicting elements—willing the good, doing the wrong—and, in the language of Ovid, "seeing and approving the better things of life, but following the worse."

Peter is the supreme example of the gospel warning: "...whoever thinks he is standing secure should take care not to fall" (1 Corinthians 10:12). In no one else is better told the fallacy of humanism, understood as self-sufficiency of a person without God, or the utter inadequacy of our own reason and our own strength to get us out of the mess we are in without periodic renewals of divine grace that come to us from God.

Because Peter is so much like us in our conflicts, he is, therefore, our greatest hope. The other apostles wrote less out of their experience than Peter. The Epistle of Paul to Timothy is exhortation; the Epistle of John is a call to brotherhood; the Epistle of James is for a practical religion; but the Epistle of Peter is the summary of his former self and might be called the "epistle of courage." In every line, in every word of that revealed document, we find Peter using his dead former self as the stepping stone by which he mounts to newness of life.

To the Peter who was sinking beneath the waves, he, the new Peter, speaks courageously: "...who by the power of God are safeguarded through faith, to a salvation that is ready to be revealed in the final time. In this you rejoice, although now for a little while you may have to suffer through various trials, so that the genuineness of your faith, more precious than gold that is perishable even though tested by fire, may prove to be for praise, glory, and honor at the revelation of Jesus Christ." (1 Peter 1:5–7).

"Now who is going to harm you if you are enthusiastic for what is good? But even if you should suffer because of righteousness, blessed are you. Do not be afraid or terrified with fear of them, but sanctify Christ as Lord in your hearts. Always be ready to give an explanation to anyone who asks you for a reason for your hope" (1 Peter 3:13–15).

No wonder Our Divine Lord, Who knows all souls in their inner being, chose as the head of His Church not John who had never denied, and who alone of all the apostles was present on the hill of Calvary, but rather chose Peter who fell and then rose again, who sinned and who then was forgiven amidst lifelong penance, in order that His Church might understand something of human weakness and sin, and bear to the millions of its souls the gospel of hope, the assurance of divine mercy.

Fittingly, then, when Peter came to the end of his lease on life, he asked not to be crucified as was Our Blessed Lord with head upright, but with head downward in the earth. Our Lord had called him the Rock of His Church, and the rock was laid where it should be—deep in the roots of creation.

On that very spot where the man of courage was crucified upside down, with his stumbling feet toward heaven, there now rises the greatest dome that was ever thrown against the vault of heaven's blue, the dome of the Basilica of St. Peter in Rome. Around it in giant letters of gold, we read the words Our Lord spoke to Peter at Caesarea Philippi: "...thou art Peter; and upon this rock I will build my church, and the gates of hell shall not prevail against it" (Matthew 16:18).

Many a time I have knelt under that dome and its inscription and looked down below its many altars to the tomb where is buried that Rock who made Rome eternal, because he the fisherman came to live there. No one, I suppose, has ever bent a suppliant knee to that first vicar of Christ's Church, to whom Our Lord said that a sinner should be forgiven, not seven times, but seventy times seven, without understanding in hope what Peter knew so well: "If you had never sinned, you never could call Christ 'Savior.'"

❦

Be strong and of a good courage; be not afraid,
neither be thou dismayed; for the Lord thy God
is with thee, wheresoever thou goest.
—JOSHUA 1:9

CHAPTER TWO

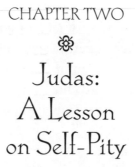

Judas:
A Lesson
on Self-Pity

The expression "fallen away" or "lapsed" refers to those who, at one time blessed with grace and intimacy with the Divine, later abandon it. Our Lord referred to them in the parable of the Sower: "[T]hey have no root; they last only for a time. Then when tribulation or persecution comes because of the word, they quickly fall away" (Mark 4:17).

No one yet has ever left the Body of Christ or His Church for a reason, but many have left it for a thing. The thing may differ: It may be pride, wealth, flesh, or the thousand-and-one substitutes for Divinity. This truth can best be illustrated by a study of Judas, the one man in the gospels who left Our Lord for a thing, and of whom Our Lord said, "It would be better for that man if he had never been born" (Matthew 26:24).

One day a babe was born at Kerioth. Friends and relatives came with gifts for the babe, because he was a child of promise. Not so far away another Babe was born in the village of Bethlehem. Because He, too, was a child of promise, friends came with gifts of gold, frankincense, and myrrh. Both babes grew in age, and one day the man of Bethlehem met the man of Kerioth at the parting of the waters, and Our Lord chose Judas as His apostle.

He was the only Judean among the apostles; and since the Judeans were more skilled in administration than the Galileans, Judas was given the apostolic purse. Probably he was naturally best fitted for the task. To use a person for what he is naturally fitted is to keep him—if he can be kept—from apostasy and alienation and dissatisfaction. But at the same time, life's temptations come often from that for which we have the greatest aptitude.

There must be first an inward failure, however, before there can be an outward one. Judas was avaricious. Avarice is a pernicious sin, for when other vices grow old, avarice is still young. The covetousness of Judas revealed itself particularly in Simon's house when an uninvited guest, a sinful woman, broke in at dinner and poured ointment over the feet of Our Lord and then wiped it away with her hair. And the house was filled with the odor of the ointment.

Judas was at dinner that day. Judas knew how near the Lord's betrayal was. Mary, that woman, knew how near His death was. Putting on the mask of charity, Judas simulated anger that such precious ointment should be wasted: "Why was not this ointment sold for three hundred pence, and given to the poor? Now he said this, not because he cared for the poor; but because he was a thief and held the money bag and used to steal the contributions." (John 12:5–6).

Our Lord did not affront Judas, who affronted Him. There is something inexpressibly sad and yet so patient, gentle, and tender in the words of Our Lord, "Leave her alone" (John 12:7). Surely there could be no waste in a ministry to Divine Love.

There will always be souls like Judas who are scandalized at the wealth offered to Christ in His Church. If a man can give jewels to the woman he loves without scandal, why cannot the soul pour out its abundance to the God it loves in tribute of affection?

Our Lord praised the woman, saying she had anointed Him for His burial. Judas was shocked! So He was going to die! A short time later, on Wednesday of Holy Week, Our Lord told the apostles what would happen. Judas heard Him say: "You know that in two days time it will be Passover, and the Son of Man will be handed over to be crucified" (Matthew 26:2).

Christ would be crucified. That was certain. In the general cataclysm Judas must rescue something to solace his acquisitive spirit. "Then one of the Twelve, who was called Judas Iscariot, went to the chief priests and said, 'What are you willing to give me if I hand him over to you?' They paid him thirty pieces of silver" (Matthew 26:14–15). Eight hundred years before Zechariah prophesied, "'If it seems good to you, give me my wages; but if not, let it go.' And they counted out my wages, thirty pieces of silver" (Zechariah 11:12). He who took the form of a servant was sold for the price of a slave.

The next evening on the occasion of Our Lord's Last Supper when He made His Last Testament, and left to us that which on dying no man ever has been able to leave, namely Himself, the Savior again spoke about His betrayal: "…One of you is about to betray me" (Matthew 26:21). The disciples looked at one another saying, "Is it I, Lord?" "Is it I?"

No conscience is pure in the sight of God; no one can be sure of his innocence. Judas then asked, "Is it I, Rabbi?" The Lord answered, "Thou hast said it." And Judas went out and "it was night." It is always night when one turns his back on God.

A few hours later Judas led a band of brigands and soldiers down the hill of Jerusalem. Though there was a full moon that night, the soldiers did not know whom they were to apprehend, so they asked Judas for a sign. Turning to them, he said, "The man I shall kiss is the one; arrest him" (Matthew 26:48).

Crossing over the brook of Kedron and into the Garden, Judas threw his arms around the neck of Our Lord and blistered His lips with a kiss. One word came back: "Friend." Then the question: "Are you betraying the Son of Man with a kiss?" (Luke 22:48). It was the last time that Jesus spoke to Judas. Judas had the right to the fatted calf, but he preferred the golden one.

Only Judas knew where to find Our Lord after dark. Soldiers did not know. Christ in His Church is delivered into the hands of the enemy from *within*. It is the bad Christians who betray. The greatest harm to the cause of Christ is not done by enemies, but by those who have been cradled in her sacred associations and nourished in the faith. The scandal of the "fallen aways" provides opportunities for enemies who still are timid. The enemies do the bloody work of crucifixion, but those who have communed with Christ prepare the way.

Judas was more zealous in the cause of the enemy than he was in the cause of Our Lord. Those who leave the Church in like manner seek to atone for their uneasy consciences by attacking the Church. Since their consciences will not leave them alone, they will not leave the Guide of their consciences alone. The Voltaire who left the Church was the Voltaire who scoffed. Their hatred is not due to their unbelief, but their unbelief is due to their hatred. The Church makes them uneasy in their sin, and they feel that. If they could drive the Church from the world they could sin with impunity.

But why betray with a kiss? Because the betrayal of

Divinity is such a heinous crime that it must always be prefaced by some mark of affection. How often in discussions of religion we hear a word of praise about Christ in His Church and then a "but" which begins the slur.

The human things we can attack without excuse; they need no pretended love to sheathe the sword that kills. But in the presence of the Sacred and the Divine, one must feign affection where affection should be unfeigned.

How many there are who attack its beliefs only because, as they say, they would keep its doctrine pure. If they assail its discipline, it is because they want to preserve a liberty or even a license that they believe essential to piety. If they accuse the Church of not being spiritual enough, it is because they claim to be defenders of the highest ideals—though none of them ever tell us how spiritual the Church must be before they would embrace it. In each instance, hostility to Divinity is preceded by a deference toward religion: "Hail, Rabbi," and he kissed him.

No sooner was the crime done than Judas was disgusted. The deep wells of remorse began surging up in his soul; but like so many souls today, he took his remorse to the wrong place. He went back to those with whom he trafficked. He had sold the Lord for thirty pieces of silver, or in our money about seventeen dollars.

Divinity is always betrayed out of all proportion to its real worth. Whenever we sell Christ, be it for worldly advancement, such as those who give up their faith because they cannot get anywhere politically with a cross on their backs, or be it for wealth, we always feel cheated in the end.

No wonder Judas took the thirty pieces of silver back to those who gave it to him, and sent the coins ringing and rolling and jingling across the Temple floor saying, "I have sinned in betraying innocent blood" (Matthew 27:4). He no longer wanted what he once wanted most. All the glamour was gone. Not even those to whom he returned the money wanted it. The money was good for nothing, except to buy a field of blood. Judas made restitution of his money; however, souls are not saved by giving up what they have, but by giving what they are.

Being disgusted with sin is not enough. We must also be repentant. The Gospel tells us, "Then Judas, his betrayer, seeing that Jesus had been condemned, deeply regretted what he had done" (Matthew 27:3). But Judas did not repent in the true sense of the word. Rather, he had a change of feeling. He *repented*, but not to Our Lord; he repented unto *himself*.

The latter is only self-hatred, and self-hatred is suicidal. To hate self is the beginning of self-slaughter. Self-hatred is salutary only when associated with the love of God.

Disillusionment and disgust may be a step toward religion, but it is not religion. Some think they love God because life did not keep all its promises, or because their dreams did not come true. They longed for an earthly part, and it turned out to be a mirage. They begin to see the vanity of the world. Depressions, sorrows, sickness, war, disappointments, have gradually weaned them from the world.

They no longer get much enjoyment from the world. They have no prospects of ever recovering their youth, so they turn to a mild hatred of sin. They confuse wisdom with satiety. They think they are pure because they are no longer tempted. They judge virtues by the vices from which they abstain. They care very little for the approval or disapproval of the world. Old friends are no longer interesting; new friends cannot be found.

The result is that in the course of time they turn to religion as a solace. They begin to keep the commandments because they have *no strong* motive for not doing it. They give up drink and other vices that may ruin their health. Their good is the good of inertia; they are like icebergs in the cold streams of the north. Because such people are full of anxiety, complexes, and fears, they begin reading Freud and learn that their emotions must in some way be sublimated. They repent, but they repent unto themselves. They are sorry for their lot, but not sorry for having offended God.

And when did the betrayal of Judas begin? The first record that we have in the gospels of Judas falling was the day when Our Blessed Lord announced that He would leave Himself to the world in the Eucharist. Inserted in that marvelous story of this great sacrament is the suggestion that Our Lord knew who would betray Him. Our Lord had just announced that He would continue His Presence in the world hidden under the form of bread.

In His own majestic words He heralded that union with Him would be more intimate than the union between the body and the food we ate: "Just as the living Father has sent me and I have life because of the Father, so also the one who feeds on me will have life because of me...whoever eats this bread will live forever" (John 6:57–58).

Our Lord, knowing what went on in human souls, added, "But there are some of you that believe not." And the Gospel adds, "Jesus knew from the beginning the ones who would not believe and the who would betray him" (John 6:64).

The actual betrayal came the very night Our Lord gave that which He promised He would give for the life of the world, namely, the Holy Eucharist.

No story in all the gospel so much reveals the power of a single passion to enwrap, enchain, possess, and degrade a person's character as the tragedy of the traitor apostle. What religious associations could have been better than those of Judas, who received into his mind, memory, and heart the impress of the one incomparable Life with its thousand radiant rays of wisdom and charity?

It is we, then, who know Him, who possess His truth and His life, who can injure Him more than those who know Him not. We may never act the traitor's part in a big way, but through insignificant signs: like the kiss of Judas, by a silence when we should defend, by fear of ridicule when we should proclaim, by a criticism when we ought to witness, or by a shrug of the shoulders when we ought to fold our hands in prayer. Well indeed may the Savior then ask us, "Friend, will you betray Me with a kiss?"

Judas went down into the valley of Ennom—the valley of ghastly associations, the Gehenna of the future. Over the cold, rocky ground he walked, amidst the jagged rocks between gnarled and stunted trees, which looked just like his twisted and tortured soul. There was only one thought in his mind: to empty himself of himself.

Everything seemed to bear witness against him. The dust was his destiny; the rocks were his heart; the trees, particularly, seemed to speak—their branches were as accusing arms and pointing fingers; their knots as so many eyes. The leaves seemed to shake in protest against making them the instrument of his vain destruction. They seemed almost to whisper that all other trees of its kind would tremble in shame until the final day of the Great Assize.

Taking a halter from his cincture—and how that cincture reminded him of Peter's cincture whence swung the keys of heaven—he threw it over a strong limb and fastened one end of the halter about his neck. The winds seemed to bring him the echo of words he heard a year before: "Come to me all you who labor and are heavily burdened and find rest for your souls." But he would repent unto himself, not to God.

And as the sun darkened, two trees made history on opposite sides of Sion—one the tree of Calvary and hope; the other, the tree of Ennom and despair. On one hung Him Who would unite heaven and earth, and on the other hung him who willed to be foreign to both.

And the pity of it all was that he might have been Saint Judas. He possessed what every soul possesses: a tremendous potential for sanctity and peace. But let us be sure that whatever be our sins, and regardless of the depths of our betrayal, there is ever a Hand outstretched to embrace, a Face shining with the light of forgiveness, and a Divine Voice that speaks a word to us, as it did with Judas even unto the end: "Friend."

❀

Love seeketh not itself to please,
Nor for itself hath any care,
But for another gives its ease,
And builds a Heaven in Hell's despair.
—WILLIAM BLAKE

CHAPTER THREE

❀

Pilate:
A Lesson on
Political Power

One wonders if there are really any new things in the world, or if only the same things are happening to different people. Take, for example, the relation of politics and religion. Those who have their finger on the pulse of contemporary civilization have probably noted that there are two contradictory charges against religion today. The first is that religion is not political enough; the other is that religion is too political. On the one hand, the Church is blamed for being too divine, and on the other, for not being divine enough. It is hated because it is too heavenly and hated because it is too earthly.

Particularly significant it is that these were the very two charges for which Christ Himself was condemned: The religious judges, Annas and Caiaphas, found Him too religious; the political judges, Pilate and Herod, found Him too political.

Caiaphas, the religious judge, standing before his judgment seat, asked, "I order you to tell us under oath before the living God whether you are the Messiah, the Son of God" (Matthew 26:63). As the question rang out through the marble hall and was succeeded by a silence vibrant with emotion, Christ finally raised His eyes to the judge and answered, "You have said so" (Matthew 26:64).

A gleam of satisfaction lighted the judge's face. At last he had triumphed! But he must not show it, and under the veil of horrified indignation at the insult offered to God's supreme majesty by declaring Himself to be God, he rent his garments from bottom to top, crying out, "He has blasphemed!" (Matthew 26:65). Christ is too religious! Too heavenly! Too infallible! Too spiritual! Too much interested in souls! Too divine!

Because He was too religious, He was not political enough. The religious judges said that He had no concern for the fact that the Romans were their masters, and that they might take away their country (John 11:47–48). By talking about a spiritual kingdom, a higher moral law, and His divinity, and by becoming the leader of a spiritual crusade, He was accused of being indifferent to the needs of the people and national well-being.

The Romans would not tolerate anyone with such an appeal. He would bring down retribution from Rome. Their armies would come and destroy them. After all, what good is religion, anyway, if it has no part in the political, economic, and social setup of a country. So Caiaphas decided: Better let the one man die rather than the whole nation should perish.

Within a few hours Our Blessed Lord, Who was accused of being too disinterested in politics, is charged with being too interested in it. The mob who had their prisoner bound with rope stopped outside Pilate's doorsill, which marked the confines of a Roman house.

Pilate, warned of their coming, went out to meet the accusers. Jesus and Pilate were face to face. Pilate looked at the Figure before him, silent and unmoved, crimsoned with His own blood, with livid red marks across His face, already the object of gross mistreatment before He had been condemned. Turning to the howling mob, Pilate asked, "What charge do you bring against this man?" (John 18:29).

If the charge was that He blasphemed by calling Himself God, Pilate would have only smiled. He had his own gods and each day sprinkled incense before them. What cared he about their divinities?

But there was one other charge about Christ that could be hurled, and it was the opposite one, namely, that He was too political, that He was not sufficiently divine, that He meddled in national affairs, that He was not patriotic. And in answer to Pilate's question, there was hurled against the balustrade of his temple the deafening roar of three charges: "We have found this man perverting our nation, and forbidding to give tribute to Caesar, and saying that he is Christ the king" (Luke 23:2).

And so throughout history, these two contradictory charges have been leveled against the Person of Christ in His Body the Church. His Church [was] accused of not being political enough when it condemn[ed] Nazism and Fascism; it is accused of being too political when it condemns Communism. It is too unpolitical when it does not condemn a political regime that some other political systems dislike but which allows religious freedom; it is said to be too political when it condemns a political regime that completely suppresses all religion.

What is the logic of these contradictory charges? Apparently, the world figures that the Church is something to be used, a rather refining influence whose sole business is to make *moral whoopee* for certain kinds of politics. When there is an accidental coincidence of the spiritual and the political as there was on Palm Sunday, then there is a moment of peace—but it is a false peace, which is the prelude to Good Friday.

It is the second charge that needs specific consideration, namely, that the Church is interfering in politics. Is this true? It all depends upon what you mean by politics. If by interference in politics is meant using influence to favor a particular regime, party, or system that respects the basic God-given rights and freedom of persons, the answer is emphatically *No!* The Church does not interfere in politics. If by interference in politics is meant judging or condemning a philosophy of life that makes the party, or the state, or the class, or the race the source of all rights, and that usurps the soul and enthrones party over conscience and denies those basic rights for which this war was fought, the answer is emphatically *Yes!* The Church does judge such a philosophy. But when it does this, it is not interfering with politics, for such politics is no longer politics but theology. When a state sets itself up as absolute as God, when it claims sovereignty over the soul, when it destroys freedom of conscience and freedom of religion, then the state has ceased to be political and has begun to be a counter-Church.

As long as politics is politics, the Church has nothing to say. It is totally indifferent to any regime. The Church adapts itself to all governments on condition that they respect liberty of conscience. It is indifferent as to whether people choose to live under a monarchy, republic, democracy, or even a military dictatorship, provided these governments grant the basic freedoms. If by "interference in politics" is meant the interference by the clergy in the political realm of the state, the Church is unalterably opposed to it, for the Church teaches that the state is supreme in the temporal order. But when politics ceases to be politics and begins to be a religion, when it claims supremacy over the human soul, when it reduces the person to a grape for the sake of the line of collectivity, when it limits his destiny to be a servant of Moloch, when it denies both the freedom of conscience and freedom of religion, when it competes with religion on its own ground, the immortal soul that is destined for God, then religion protests. And when it does, its protest is not against politics but against a counter-religion that is anti-religious.

A human organism can adapt itself to the torrid heat of the equator or to the glacial cold of the North, but it cannot live without air. In like manner, the Church can adapt itself to every form of politics, but it cannot live without the air of freedom. Never before in history has the spiritual been so unprotected against the political. Never before has the political so usurped the spiritual. It was Jesus Christ Who suffered under Pontius Pilate; it was not Pontius Pilate who suffered under Jesus Christ.

The grave danger today is not religion in politics but politics in religion. For the first time in Christian history, politics, which began by divorcing itself from morality and religion, has seen that man cannot live by bread alone. So it has attempted to capture his soul, by every word that proceeds from the mouth of a dictator. For the first time in Western Christian civilization, the kingdom of anti-God has acquired political form and social substance, and stands over and against Christianity as a counter-Church with its own dogmas, its own scriptures, its own infallibility, its own hierarchy, its own visible head, its own missionaries, and its own invisible head—too terrible to be named.

In certain countries today religion exists only by sufferance of a political dictator. Without actively persecuting the Church, it usurps its functions, gives bread cards only to those who conspire against religion, attempts to create an ideological uniformity by liquidating anyone who is opposed to that ideology, and by sheer weight of state-inspired propaganda would effect the mass organization of society on a purely secular and antireligious basis.

Culture today is becoming politicized. The modern state is extending dominance over areas outside its province, family, education, and the soul. It is concentrating public opinion in fewer and fewer hands, which becomes the more dangerous because of the mechanical way in which propaganda can be disseminated. It seeks to achieve its ends by extra-parliamentary means. The idea of a community of workers is replaced by mass cooperation on a nonpersonal basis; contract has taken the place of responsibility. The lines are becoming clear-cut.

The conflict of the future will be between a God-religion and a state-religion, between Christ and anti-Christ in political disguise.

History attests that religion has not encroached upon the temporal sphere, but rather jealous temporal rulers have invaded the spiritual arena. Sometimes these rulers were kings and princes, even so-called "Catholic defenders of the faith." Today they are dictators.

But the problem is ever the same—the invasion of the spiritual by the political. If it be objected that religion once made Henry come to Canossa, let it be stated that it was for exactly the same reason that the world made war against Hitler, namely, because of his usurpation of spiritual freedom. The difference between Henry's time and Hitler's is that when religion had some influence in the world and kings had consciences, it was possible for the Church to inspire them to penance. With that moral authority rejected, now the nations have to spend five-hundred-and-twenty-three billion dollars and millions of lives to impress some of the dictators with the same fact.

There is something alarming about that brief description of how Our Lord died. No other name is mentioned in the Creed except the name of one judge—Judas, Annas, and Caiaphas are not mentioned. The earthly life of Our Lord is quickly passed over, but one significant detail is retained: "He suffered under Pontius Pilate." This is a record not only of an historical fact but also a prophecy of what will happen to Christ in His Mystical Body from time to time: Namely, His Church in the dark days of history will go down to a seemingly final death and persecution, suffering under Pontius Pilate—the power of an omnipotent state.

It may do religion no good to oppose state-religion, for the modern state is armed and the Church is not. Religion may even be buffeted between an ancient judge who thinks that it is expedient that one man die rather than the whole nation perish, and a modern judge who feels that it is expedient that all the people should die for one man who is a dictator. It may hear from the lips of modern Pilates the words of power: "Do you not know that I have the power to condemn you?" But there will always come back to them the soft voice of Christ: "You would have no power unless it were given to you from above."

Even though Christ Himself would not deliver us from the power of the totalitarian state, as He did not deliver Himself, we must see His purpose in it all. Maybe His children are being persecuted by the world in order that they might withdraw themselves from the world. Maybe His most violent enemies may be doing His work negatively, for it could be the mission of totalitarianism to preside over the liquidation of a modern world that became indifferent to God and His moral laws.

Maybe those of us who did not care whether God exists or not may yet suffer from those whom we taught—through the works of Feuerbach and Hegel, for example—to exile Him altogether. Maybe the very secularism from which we suffer is a reaction against our own spiritual infirmity. Maybe the growth of atheism and totalitarianism is the measure of our want of zeal and piety and the proof of our unfulfilled Christian duties.

Not until we bear the marks of Christ will we be liberated in His victory. Maybe those Christians who in the last century identified religion with naive optimism and

translated Darwinism into economic language of an un-
limited prosperity must yet learn that Christ is not of the
times, lest He should perchance be widowed by the times.

Maybe it is our loss of supernatural standards, our
decline of the family, our want of reverence for others,
our growing selfishness, that have made this state of affairs possible. Maybe we are to learn the hard way that
our destiny is not to be found in the dimensions of temporal history, for the Church is, as Newman said, "a universal Empire without earthly arms; temporal pretensions
without temporal sanctions; a claim to rule without the
power to enforce; a continual tendency to acquire with a
continual exposure to be dispossessed; greatness of mind
with weakness of body."

But whatever be the reason for these trying days, of this
we may be certain: The Christ Who suffered under
Pontius Pilate signed Pilate's death warrant; it was not
Pilate who signed Christ's. Christ's Church will be at-
tacked, scorned, and ridiculed, but it will never be destroyed.
The enemies of God will never be able to dethrone the
heavens of God, nor to empty the tabernacles of their
Eucharistic Lord, nor to cut off all absolving hands, but
they may devastate the earth.

The bald fact the enemies of God must face is that
modern civilization has conquered the world, but in doing so has lost its soul. And in losing its soul it will lose
the very world it gained. Even our own so-called liberal
culture in the United States, which has tried to avoid com-

plete secularization by leaving little zones of individual freedom, is in danger of forgetting that these zones were preserved only because religion was in their soul. And as religion fades so will freedom, for only where the spirit of God is, is there liberty.

Politics has become so all-possessive of life, that by impertinence it thinks the only philosophy a person can hold is the right or the left. This question puts out all the lights of religion so they can call all the cats gray. It assumes that man lives on a purely horizontal plane, and can move only to the right or the left. Had we eyes less material, we would see that there are two other directions where a man with a soul may look: the vertical directions of "up" or "down."

Both figured in the crucifixion of Our Lord. Even those cruel men who crucified knew that these were the directions that counted. So they shouted to Him: "Come down," and we will believe. Somehow or other that echo has been caught up and it is being bruited about the world today. "Down with religion!" "Down with capital!" "Down with labor!" "Down with reactionaries!" "Down with progressives!"

Have we not been tearing down long enough? Can one build a world with the word "down"? Is there no other cry in our vocabulary? Did not the Captain Christ give another: "If I be lifted up, I will draw all things to myself."

Lifted up! Who shall lift us up? Crucifying dictators?

Maybe! But where shall we be lifted? To the cross, the prelude of the empty tomb, the cross of Christ our Redeemer. Hear that word "up." Shout it abroad! "Up from class hatred; up from envy; up from avarice; up from war; up beyond the margin of the world; up beyond the 'troubled gateways of the stars'—UP...UP...UP to God!"

❀

*It is as hard and severe a thing
to be a true politician as to be truly moral.*
—FRANCIS BACON

CHAPTER FOUR

❀

Herod:
A Lesson on
Self-Love

I s it possible for a soul to have too many opportunities for conversion, so that in the end he becomes blinded by the very Light that should have illumined his path to God? Herod gives the answer.

His capital was at Tiberias about fifteen miles from Nazareth and ten miles from Capernaum, along the sea of Galilee where Our Lord spent so much of His ministry. Herod must have heard much of Our Lord, not only because of the smallness of his kingdom, but also because the gospel tells us that Joan, the wife of Herod's steward, was healed of evil spirits by Our Lord and afterward "ministered" to the itinerant Jesus and His apostles by surrendering her wealth. We read in Acts that Manahen, a "foster brother" of Herod, became one of the first Christian teachers in Antioch. The influence of Our Lord at least entered into Herod's household and friendships, even though it did not penetrate his heart.

Two episodes lay bare the soul of Herod. The first, his divorce from his wife and his second marriage to Herodias, who was his brother's wife and also the daughter of his half-brother Aristobulus. As our modern world would put it, "There was incompatibility between Herod and his first wife, but he and Herodias had so many things in common."

The second revealing act of Herod is his treatment of John the Baptist. He had invited John the Baptist into his palace not to hear the truth of his preaching but to enjoy the thrill of his oratory. There are so many in the world that way: They do not want to be better; they want only to feel better. But John was not the type of preacher who toned down his gospel to suit the paganism of his hearers. Because he condemned Herod's second marriage, he lost his head. Everyone in the world at one time loses his head, but it is better to lose one's head John's way in the defense of truth, rather than Herod's way, in wine and passion.

After John's decapitation, Herod heard of Jesus, and thought Jesus might be John's avenging spirit come back to haunt him. Full of superstition he thought that it was

John risen from the dead. "Now Herod, the tetrarch, heard of all things that were done by him; and he was in a doubt, because it was said by some, that John was risen from the dead; but by others that Elias had appeared; and by still others, that one of the old prophets was risen again. And Herod said, 'John I have beheaded; but who is this of whom I hear such things?' And he sought to see him" (Luke 9:7–9).

Thus do people who have no religion become addicts of superstition. After the execution of John the Baptist, Our Lord withdrew in the desert. "The same day, there came some of the Pharisees, saying to him: Depart and get thee hence, for Herod hath a mind to kill thee. And He said to them, 'Go and tell that fox, Behold, I cast out devils, and do cures today and tomorrow, and the third day I am consummated. Nevertheless I must walk today and tomorrow, and the day following, because it cannot be that a prophet perish, out of Jerusalem'" (Luke 13:31–33).

Recall that Pilate was the governor of the southern Kingdom of Judea while Herod was the tetrarch of the northern Kingdom of Israel. During the trial before Pilate, Our Lord was charged with being too political. Pilate, after examining Our Lord, went out to the porch of the Temple and said to the Lord's accusers: "I find no cause in this man" (Luke 23:4). That should have been the end of the trial. But the multitude shot back, "He stirs up the people, teaching throughout all Judea, beginning from Galilee to this place" (Luke 23:5).

Galilee! How Pilate seized upon that word. If Our Lord were from Galilee then He was not under Pilate's jurisdiction. It was a diplomatic stroke of political opportunism. As a Galilean He was under the jurisdiction of Herod, and Herod was in Jerusalem that very day for the Paschal season. Off to Herod He must go. It was "good politics," which means it was expedient, but morally it was downright dishonesty and knavery.

Herod had all the vices of his father—cruel, avaricious, dissipated—but not his genius for cunning. He was an Edomite, and the Edomites were the descendants of Esau who had sold his birthright to Jacob for a mess of porridge, and who thus had become the father to a people who loved more than valued things of this earth.

Esau is recorded in Scripture as the type of sensual man who did not rise above the animal, and whose epitaph is written in the New Testament: "Lest there be any fornicator, or profane person, as Esau; who for one mess, sold his first birth right" (Hebrews 12:16). Nowhere in the Old Testament do we hear of Edomite gods or Edomite religion. They were people without conscience, living on spoils and vengeance. Their one quality was shrewdness, and Our Lord stamped their race with it when He called Herod a fox (Luke 13:32).

Our Lord now stands before the fox, the traitor, incestuous adulterer, assassin of John, enemy of the people, the most fitting person in the world to condemn innocence. That Babe of Bethlehem Whom his father tried to kill now stands manacled before Herod. "And Herod seeing Jesus, was very glad; for he was desirous of a long time to see him, because he had heard many things of him; and he hoped to see some sign wrought by him" (Luke 23:8).

Herod was glad! But glad only because he hoped to see a trick. He would compel Our Lord to display some magic to save His life. This is all religion means to some people: a passing delectation to get them over a moment in the intolerable boredom of life. It makes them feel good between satieties. Herod's court was there; his bodyguard, courtesans, sycophants, and probably Herodias and Salome, whose hands were still wet with the blood of the Baptist.

Herod began by asking Our Lord many questions, not questions of doctrine and discipline as Annas had done, but questions prompted by curiosity. Jaded souls present intellectual difficulties, never pleas for moral regeneration. Therefore to all the questions Our Lord answered him nothing. He tried to save Judas and Pilate, but for Herod—not a word.

Why did Our Lord refuse to speak to Herod? Can it be that He who came to save all men and Who loved them enough to die for them, should still not *even try* to win calloused souls *like Herod?* Why should He Who spoke to Judas the traitor, Magdalen the harlot, and the thief, now be silent before a king?

Because the conscience of Herod was dead. He was too familiar with religion. He wanted miracles, yes, but not to surrender his will, but to satisfy his curiosity. His soul was already so blunted by appeals, including even the Baptist's, that another appeal would only have intensified his guilt. He was stone deaf on the side of God. He was as one dead in body and soul, eaten by luxury and sin. Herod was not offering his soul for salvation, but only his nerves for titillation.

Spiritualized sensation-hunting is not religion. Christ is no minister to the senses. The capacity for holiness had been killed in Herod.

So the Lord of the universe spoke not a word to the worldling. Nero had the conscience of Seneca to guide him, but it did not restrain his lust and cruelty. Alexander had Aristotle, but it did not temper his imperialism. Herod the Great had the Wise Men, but it did not hinder his butchery. Herod his son had John the Baptist, but it did not prevent his mockery of religion.

Herod stands as the type of those who have already had enough knowledge about religion, but refuse to do anything about it. The Scripture describes them: "Because they have hated instruction, and received not the fear of the Lord." "Then shall they call upon me, and I will not hear" (Proverbs 1:29, 28).

Men have spoken of hell in various images but none are more terrible than the image of the silence of God. "...O my God, be not thou silent to me: lest if thou be silent to me, I become like them that go down into the pit" (Psalms 28:1).

God sometimes judges in silence. And that silence of

Our Lord clamored more in Herod's ear than did the loud rebuke of John the Baptist. Such silence is thunder, for it is the penalty God inflicts on the soul that is not sincere or that looks for a truth not to embrace but to reject.

Probably the worst punishment God can visit upon a soul is to leave it alone. Then no sound, no ruffled conscience, no reproach. "Ephraim is joined to his idols! Let him alone." Nature speaks to us in the reproachful language of pain when we violate its laws, for example, break a bone. A toothache proves nature has a tongue bidding us remedy the evil. Conscience too has a voice; it bids us turn back again to God with every remorse.

But there are some diseases that kill without the voice of pain—the cancer that destroys in silence. So too with conscience. If it no longer speaks in remorse, think not that you are healthy. Your soul may be dead. Our Lord will answer you nothing then, even when you robe Him as a fool. Then the hush about the cross to which you have sent Him will be His last appeal.

This is the punishment, too, of the secular spirit of the modern world. Its soul has become dead to religion. Religion has become to the modern mind a vulgar curiosity. Beware of a dead conscience, of turning dead ears to the thousand-and-one actual graces that come to you in a month to turn to God, to seek the truth, to purge your conscience. Beware of that moral trifling which seals the lips of God, because there is nothing in such a soul where the spirit of God can operate.

Woe to those who boast their consciences are clear when they are really dead. Tell them of a fault or a duty undone, and they reply confidently that it does not trouble them. Regardless of what others may think, the sin is not on their consciences. Well may they search their souls and ask if their peace be not the false deadly peace of the devil's palace where he dwells with all his armor. "When a strong man armed keepeth his court, those things are in peace which he possesseth" (Luke 11:21).

There does come a time every now and then in history when the moral judgments of religion on an outmoded society fall on dead ears: "They have ears and hear not." What good does it do today for religion to tell the modern world that divorce and the breakdown of family life will end in the destruction of the nation? Who will listen to us if we say that a state that persecutes religion is a menace to the world? Who heeds the warning to capitalists that the privacy of profits is wrong when the principles of social justice are ignored and to labor leaders that organization is not an end but only a means to the common good of a nation?

The dead consciences have only one reaction to religion, and it is the same as the reaction of Herod, namely, mockery which seemingly gives them intellectual superiority. By regarding others as beneath one's intelligence, one seems to put himself above their intelligence.

This brings us to the second act in the drama of Herod: the robing of Christ in the garment of a fool and sending

Him back to Pilate. In Rome when a man was a candidate for office he clad himself in a white robe—*toga candida,* whence comes our word "candidate"—and went from elector to elector seeking suffrage. Perhaps by robing Him thus, Herod meant to suggest here was a candidate for kingship and divinity, but a candidate whose claims were receiving little support either from a procurator or a tetrarch.

It was a good joke. He could trust Pilate to see the humor of it. It would serve a double purpose; it would prove Christ was a fool, and when Pilate and he would laugh over it they would be friends, for when men laugh together, enmity ceases, even when the butt of the humor is God.

Wicked power cannot stand the vision of an innocent conscience. From the days of youth when the good boy is ridiculed by bad boys, because his goodness is a judgment passed upon them, to the days of maturity when evil men ridicule religion, the moral is ever the same: Religious persecution arises in the world not because religion is corrupt, but because consciences are corrupt.

One of the penalties of being religious is to be mocked and ridiculed. If Our Lord submitted Himself to the ribald humor of a degenerate tetrarch, we may be sure that we, His followers, will not escape. The more divine a religion is, the more the world will ridicule you, for the spirit of the world is the enemy of Christ. Purely humanistic religions and popular sects founded by emotional moderns are never the object of the world's scorn. But once a religion lays claim to being divine, then it must be prepared to accept the contumely of that which is not divine. Then laughter and humor, which are so necessary to human existence, become downright wicked because they are turned against Him Who gave them.

Now look at the ridicule of religion from the side of those who inflict it. There it exacts a terrible penalty, for it blinds the scoffer to his greatest need and to his own salvation. It is very much like a starving man who scoffs at a neighbor who gives him food because the neighbor happens to be poorly clad.

The tragedy of religious mockery is that it rejects Him Who alone can save. Herod rejected his own peace in ridiculing the Prisoner before him. They, too, who offer no intellectual opposition but who turn to ridicule everything that pertains to religion, and who laugh at the saved and sneer at the holy, shall go out into the night unblessed and weeping.

Our present moment is something like that in which the conscience of Our Lord stood impotent before Herod. We are being robed in the garment of a fool. We are mocked if we preach Christ's teaching. We are called fools if we ask for the restoration of religion to education; fools if we affirm that all political power is from God; fools if we insist that world unity is impossible without a recognition of a universal moral law; fools if we pray, if we fast, if we discipline ourselves.

And there is the answer: Fools we must be as Christ

was mocked as a fool. An era of sensuality is necessarily an era of persecution. An age of unreason is an age of mockery. Wicked power will not submit to the judgment of truth. Bring out, then, your white robes of mockery, O Lord, as you did to Christ, that You may show the great gulf that is fixed between You and the servants of the Spirit. Take on that robe of a fool, fellow Christians, for a new crime is arising in the world, the crime of being a Christian. Your Christ has worn the robe of a fool before you: "But God chose the foolish of the world to shame the wise" (1 Corinthians 1:27).

His robe of glory in heaven is white, too. The Book of the Apocalypse tells us that the robe of the martyr is white. Let the soldiers take this white robe of Herod and raffle it off with the shake of dice. Thy robes of glory will be white, not as mock symbols of candidacy for political power, but as the glorious badge of the children of the Lamb. Be not cast down as you wear the robe. You will be hated for a time: "I have chosen you out of the world, therefore the world hates you" (John 15:19). "In the world you shall have distress" (John 16:33).

Divinity is the one thing in the world before which people cannot remain long indifferent. They must either love or hate. Christ is too big to be ignored, too holy to be unhated. What the evil spirits said of Him could be put into the lips of everyone who works evil: "What have we to do with the Jesus of Nazareth. Are you come to destroy us?"

Evil is too hypersensitive to be indifferent to the challenge of the good. It knows its enemies long in advance. Let anyone come into the world who believes in Freud and preach: "Blessed are the clean of heart"; or come to those who believe in the class struggle of Red Fascism and preach: "If any man take your cloak, give Him also your coat"; or come into a world of aggressiveness and say: "Blessed are the meek"; or into a world where children are raised without a prayer or a thought of God and say: "Suffer little children to come unto Me"; or let him drive the capitalists into the sea even though it restores a man to health, and see if he can have any other end than the cross. You cannot preach goodness to an evil world and expect anything less than to be crucified.

No one will waste time over trivia. No one will draw swords against weaklings. The instinct of evil is infallible; it knows its enemies. Look, then, for the hated Christ who is paid the beautiful tribute of opposition, the high compliment of hate. For if the world hates, then it is unworldly, and if it is unworldly, then it is divine, and if it is divine, then it is the channel of salvation.

Deny not your Master even under opposition. "But he that shall deny me before men, I will also deny him before my Father Who is in heaven" (Matthew 10:33). So long as we are hated, we are worth troubling about. The church that would give only a moral tone to secular movements can die of its own inanition. If the pagan forces of the world left us untouched, if they did not calumniate us, seek to destroy us, set up rival claimants to the soul, it would mean that we would have lost our influence, that our touch was gone, our stars no longer shone.

Do men shake fists over the tomb of Napoleon? Do armies storm and rage against the grave of Mohammed? Do forces assault the tomb of Lenin? These men are dead. But they do storm the citadel of Christ; they do rage against His Spouse; they do kill the members of His Body; they do try to stifle the young hearts that would breathe His name in school. Therefore Christ must be alive today in His Body which is the Church.

The Church can still make the evil forces of the world angry. It can still inspire persecution. Therefore Christ is with us. The exhilaration of being counted a foe of evil is the joy of honor. Our heart is warmed by the tribute of enmity from those areas of life, where to be counted friends, or not to be counted at all, would be to stand condemned as salt without savor, and as feeble candles whose lights had gone out.

And in this connection, too, one may see in the persecution of the Jews in Europe a sign of divine predilection. They may not understand the metaphysics of persecution, but it is interesting that within this century forces are at work that would persecute both Old and New Testament. Two classes have been hated; those who bore Christ and those who bear Him; those who prepared for His coming and those who follow after him. Few Christians and Jews may understand the metaphysics of modern antireligion, but deep souls among both can see and understand its meaning. There are forces afoot in the world that would have nothing to do with those who have ever had anything to do with God, and under a common enemy both are being drawn together in the embrace of the loving God who made us both.

No. Christ did not court opposition; neither does His Body which is the Church. He offered love now and then, but the selfish do not want that love, and out of it comes the opposition. While the Church gives love to all, it can test the virility of its loves by the fires of resistance that it enkindles in the breasts of all who know that Christ's love regnant spells disaster to their evil ways.

The white robe of the fool is a judgment on the world; it is the sign of its evil; the death rattle of its wickedness. Because men mock, a verdict is passed on them; because the Church is martyred by evil powers, a sentence has been pronounced on those powers. Their deeds are known to be sinful by what they do to innocence. Thus will men who live in the world and do not know where to look for religion finally find it in the religion which their very world crucified, and in finding it will find peace which the world cannot take away!

True followers of Christ, be prepared to have a world make jokes at your expense. You can hardly expect a world to be more reverent to you than to Our Lord. When it does make fun of your faith, its practices, abstinences, and rituals, then you are moving to a closer identity with

Him Who gave us our faith. Nor may you repay sneer with sneer. We cannot fight God's battles with the weapons of Satan. Repaying jeer with jeer is not the response of a Christian, for under scorn Our Lord "answered nothing." The world gets more of its amusement from a Christian who fails to be Christian, but none from his respectful silence.

The answer of Our Lord to Herod was that Our Lord continued to be Our Lord. Dogs bay at the moon all night, but the moon gives back no snarl. It goes on shining. Shine forth in thy white robe of mockery, O Christian! One day it will be the robe of your glory!

❁

Uneasy lies the head that wears a crown.
—SHAKESPEARE

Blessed are they who hunger and thirst
after righteousness, for they shall be filled.
—MATTHEW 5:6

CHAPTER FIVE

❀

Claudia and Herodias: A Lesson in Opposites

One of the most revolutionary and as yet unnoticed changes in the postwar world is the role assigned to women. Winning the world to Christ—or winning it to anti-Christ—requires playing one of two roles: that of Eve or Mary.

On October 21, 1945, the Holy Father (Pope Pius XII) published an encyclical on "Woman's Duties in Social and Political Life," and on November 26, the Communists, who [had] moved their international revolutionary setup to Paris to disclaim responsibility for a double game, called an International Women's Congress in that city.

The Christian appeal was concerned with "maintaining and strengthening the dignity of women" who well may ask "if they can hope for their real well-being from a regime dominated by capitalism" on the one hand, or from "a totalitarian state, by whatever name it would be called that would snatch away the education of their children." It outlined a program for the Christian education of women for social and political life under "the standard of Christ the King and the patronage of His wonderful Mother" in order that they might be the "restorers of honor, family, and society."

The anti-Christian appeal as presented in an authoritative pamphlet written by the German Communist woman leader, Clara Zetkin, in preparation for this congress, quoted a statement of Lenin made to her concerning "non-party International Women's Congress." "We must win over to our side the millions of toiling women...for the Communist transformation of society...the object of which is the seizing of power by establishing the proletarian dictatorship....Just imagine those who will meet with the so-called 'hyenas of the revolution,' and if all goes well, under their leadership—honest, tame, social democratic women; pious Christian women blessed by the Pope, or swearing by Luther; daughters of Privy Councillors; lady-like English pacifists, and passionate French pacifists." How well this succeeded in Paris could be verified by reading the names of those who attended—even from our own democratic United States.

Clara Zetkin continues: "Of course, Communist women must be not only the driving, but also the leading force in the preparatory work. Communist slogans and Communist proposals must be the center of the work of the Congress and of public attention. After the Congress, they must be spread among the widest possible masses of women and help to determine international mass action on the part of women."

Thus it would seem that the women of the world are to be divided as they were in the gospel times, either for the God of the heavens and the freedom rooted in the Spirit, or else for the cause of anti-Christ and the beheading of those who would proclaim the moral law in the palace of the dictators. These two roles were foreshadowed in Claudia and Herodias.

Claudia was the youngest daughter of Julia, the daughter of Caesar Augustus. Julia was married three times, the last time to Tiberius. Because of her dissolute life, Julia was exiled when she bore Claudia to a Roman knight.

When Claudia was thirteen, Julia sent her to be brought up by Tiberius. When she was sixteen, Pontius Pilate, himself of low origin, met Claudia and asked Tiberius for permission to marry her. Thus Pilate married into the emperor's family, which assured his political future. And on the strength of it Pilate was made the procurator of Judea.

Roman governors were forbidden to take their wives

with them to the provinces. Most politicians were very happy about this, but not Pilate. Love broke a stern Roman law. After Pilate was in Jerusalem six years, he sent for Claudia, who was more than eager to face the loneliness of life away from the capital of the world and amidst an unknown and alien people.

We may reasonably conclude that Claudia must have heard of Jesus, perhaps from the Jewish maid who prepared her bath, or the stewards who brought news about Him. She might actually have seen Him, for the Fortress of Antonia where she lived was near the Temple of Jerusalem, and Jesus was often there.

She might even have heard His message, and since "no man ever spoke as this man," her own soul was stirred. The very contrast between Him and His ideas of the world she knew, and the thoughts she thought, deepened His appeal. How little did the women of Jerusalem who saw Claudia looking out through the lattice, who tried to catch the flash of gems on her white hands, or mark the pride of her patrician face, ever guess how deep were her thoughts, how intense her sorrow, how profound her yearning.

We must remember that there was almost a Prussian submission to law among the Romans. No woman was allowed to interfere in the processes of law, nor even to offer a suggestion concerning legal procedure. What makes her entrance onto the scene all the more remarkable is that she sent a message to her husband, Pontius Pilate, the very day he was deciding on the most important case of his career, and the only one for which he ever will be remembered—the trial of Our Blessed Lord.

To send a message to a judge while he was in court was a punishable offense, and only the awfulness of the deed she saw about to be done could have moved Claudia to it. As Matthew records it: "And as he was sitting in the place of judgment, his wife sent to him saying, 'Have thou nothing to do with that just man; for I have suffered many things this day in a dream because of him'" (Matthew 27:19). While the women of Israel were silent, this heathen woman bore witness to the innocence of Jesus, and asked her husband to deal with Him in a righteous way.

The message of Claudia was an epitome of all that Christianity would do for pagan womanhood. She is the only Roman woman in the gospels, and she is a *woman of the very highest rank*. This dream was an epitome of the dreams and longings of a pagan world, its agelong hope for a righteous man—a Savior. It was reminiscent of a Sophocles: "Look not for any end moreover to this curse until some God appear to take upon his head the pangs of thine own sins vicarious," and of a Prometheus who "hast loved man too much."

Claudia had an imperfect knowledge of Christ, whom she called "that just man." And in this sense, too, it was the expression of the pagan world. The best things, it would seem, were preserved in the heart of a woman. She had a talent for spiritual alertness.

There was probably a time when Pilate would have

done anything his wife asked. But this time he did not. The trial reveals that the political man was wrong and the unpolitical woman was right, for Claudia better than Pilate caught the portents of the hour. Christ suffered under Pontius Pilate. But to the glory of Claudia a woman's voice was raised in the name of justice.

Now look on Herodias, the second wife of Herod, more correctly known as Herod Phillip, the son of old Herod the Great who ordered the massacre of the infants of Bethlehem. When old Herod died he left most of his fortune to her husband Phillip but without the kingship, which ill suited the woman's ambitions.

It happened that when her husband's half-brother Herod Antipas (among the eight sons of Herod the Great, three bore the name of Herod) came to visit Phillip, a love intrigue began between Herodias and her half-brother. Herod Antipas put away his wife, the daughter of Aretas, the King of Arabia, and married his brother's wife and took her to his palace, the Golden House at Machaerus. Herod was fond of lionizing strangers and particularly liked to hear great preachers. Accordingly he invited John the Baptist to preach in his court. John was not the kind of man to miss an opportunity to bring Herod and Herodias face to face with their guilty consciences. Little did they imagine the theme that the man of God would choose as his message in that Golden House. As soon as he stood before the court, he pointed an accusing finger at Herod who had married a divorced woman and thundered, "It is not lawful for you to have your brother's wife" (Mark 6:18).

Herodias winced; Herod rebelled. Freedom of spirit does not mean the right to judge another man's conscience. Before John knew it there were irons about his arms and the prison door of the underground dungeon closed in the face of the one whom Our Lord described as "the greatest man ever born of woman."

A man sometimes forgets these incidents, a woman never. A short time later came Herod's birthday. The scene is the grim castle of Machaerus, one of the most desolate places in the world, built on the top of an isolated crag of black basalt, thirty-five-hundred feet above the Dead Sea's eastern shore.

A great Baltasarian feast is planned. In the brilliantly lighted banquet hall Herod's company is gathered: lords, ladies, military authorities, hangers-on, sycophants, and rabble that always gather before a court. The castle is aglow with light; the noise of revelry penetrates into a deep dungeon below where the prisoner of Christ waits.

Finally, Herod has nothing more to offer his satiated guests in the way of excitement. Therefore, let the stimulus of a sensuous dance complete it, and let the dancer be the fair young daughter of Herodias by her first husband. The food is rich, the wine runs freely, and while they drink, Salome, the daughter of Herodias, dances. That a princess of the proud Herodian house should demean herself by dancing like a slave girl publicly in the presence of half-intoxicated men is surprising. For a woman to enter such a crowd was contrary to Oriental ideas of decency. It is not incredible, however, to those who know anything of the morals of Herod and his family.

Herod, half drunk with wine and over-effected by the dance, says to Salome: "Ask of me whatever you wish, and I will grant it to you…even to half of my kingdom." And she goes out and says to her mother, "What shall I ask?" Herodias replies, "The head of John the Baptist." And she went with haste to the king, and asked saying, "I want you to give me at once on a platter the head of John the Baptist" (Mark 6:22–25).

What would Herod do? The Gospel said Herod was "grieved" (Mark 6:26). But he had sworn to the maiden and must keep his promise. Some prefer to be unfaithful to God or to their conscience rather than be untrue to a half-drunken oath.

The guests hear the dungeon door open…. A few minutes later the gory head of John the Baptist is brought to the maiden on a silver platter, and she gives the ghastly dish to her mother.

It is amazing the similarity at first glance between Claudia and Herodias. Both were noblewomen, both the wives of politicians. Both came in contact with the greatest religious personages of all times: Claudia with Christ, Herodias with John the Baptist. Both sent messages to their husbands, and yet their reactions were so different: One served Christ, the other a totalitarian dictator.

Why was religion so distasteful to one, and so dear to the other? Why does one react to the defense of religion, and the other to an offense against it? Why does one seek to save a life, the other to take it?

Everyone in life has at least one great moment to come to God. How each of us reacts depends on whether we have a background of good will or bad will. In some there is a will to sin, occasional good actions being the interruptions to an abiding evil intention. In others there is a good will; and though a bad action may occasionally cut a tangent across it, the will, being good, is ready to make amends and make all sacrifices to follow the directives of conscience and the actual graces of the moment.

Now Claudia had a good will, Herodias an evil will. The one embraced religion, the other rejected it. The good will is like the good soil. When the seed of God's grace falls on it, it sprouts. The evil will is like the rock, it is incapable of conversion. "And some other [seed] fell upon the rock, and as soon as it was sprung up, it withered away, because it had no moisture" (Luke 8:6).

Claudia and Herodias are the prototypes of all women who have a role to play in the social and political life of the world. Women will be either the daughters of Herodias, wrecking their own homes by divorce, educating their children like Salome in the false wisdom of how to solicit men to do their worst, aligning themselves with any political leader who will further their own interests or pamper their own ambitions, who will never forget the just rebukes of modern Johns, and never scruple at being Beasts of Belchen to behead the heralds of Christ.

Or women today will be the daughters of Claudia, challenging politics when it would send righteous men to death, urging the path of highest duty when indecision, cowardice, and compromise allure; being to a husband an unfailing preacher of righteousness, his counselor, and his savior; even braving stern law rather than be unfaithful to conscience; and never scrupling to talk about the just and righteous Christ even when its penalty might well be the spurning of a love with power, but whose chaste conversation coupled with fear would almost win a governor to Christ.

Men have not been particularly successful in modern times in making a good world. Whether women will succeed in doing it will depend on whether they will bring out the best that is in men or bring out the worst.

In the Doge's Palace in Venice there is a fresco covering the entire wall of the Council Hall. The artist put his wife's face three times into the fresco, and in each case in the forefront, conspicuous in her robe of blue. Once she looks out from heaven with a saintly purity on her face; once from purgatory, with a worried and pained glance; and once from hell with the horror of unrepentant agony. What is the meaning of this anomaly?

The answer is to be found in the life of the artist. At times his wife was the good angel, to lead him Godward and heavenward. At times she was his trial, his cross, and his purgatory. And at other times she was his temptress, an agent of Satan leading him to hell.

The level of any civilization is the level of its womanhood. What Claudia was, that Pilate could be; what Herodias was, that Herod was. It is love, rather than knowledge, that makes the world. Knowledge is broken down to suit the mind to which the knowledge is given. That is why we have to give examples to children.

Love always goes out to meet the demands of the object loved. If the one loved is virtuous, we must be virtuous to win it. Hence the higher the love, the loftier must be those who pursue; the nobler the woman, the nobler the world.

When the sacred fires of a common tenderness are melting twin souls predestined for their flame, each can often make of the other whatever is ardently desired.

The mere buckling of a knight's armor by a feminine hand was not just a caprice of romanticism; it was the type of an eternal trust. The soul's armor is never well set on a man except by the one whom the man will respect when in danger of losing his honor.

Men we need, yes, strong men like Peter who will let the broad stroke of their challenge ring out on the shield of the world's hypocrisies; strong men like Paul, who with a two-edged sword will cut away the ties that bind down the energies of the world; strong men like John who with a loud voice will arouse the world from the sleek dream of unheroic repose.

But we need women, too, who in the language of the Holy Father "will be a teacher-guide to one's sisters, to direct ideas, dissipate prejudices, clarify obscure points, explain and diffuse the teachings of the Church, hold back those currents which threaten the home; for who better than she can understand what is needed for the dignity of woman, the integrity and honor of the young girl, and the protection and education of the child."

If this is the kind of woman you are, we salute you and toast you; not as the modern woman who descended from Herodias, once our superior, now our equal, but as the Christian woman—inspired by Claudia—closest to the cross on Good Friday and first at the tomb on Easter morn!

❀

God is truth, and whoever seeks the truth
is seeking God, whether they know it or not.
—BL. EDITH STEIN

Blessed are the pure in heart,
for they will see God.
—MATTHEW 5:8

CHAPTER SIX

✿

Barabbas and the Thieves: A Lesson on True Freedom

We live in an era of revolutions, but the problem is which kind of revolution shall we espouse. Like all eras, ours has its catchwords and foremost among them is the word "freedom." It may well be that as people talk most about their health when they are sick, so too they talk most about freedom when they are most in danger of losing it. When is a person free? When he is without law or restraint or when he attains the purpose for which he was made? For an answer to these questions we turn to the Eternal Drama of the Cross.

A prison can house the innocent as well as the guilty. During the rule of an invader it is possible that more innocent than guilty will be imprisoned behind bars. But without passing on the morality of the prisoners, the low, dark prison under Pilate's fortress held many a captive soul. Among them there were three who attract our attention. The name of one we know—Barabbas. The names of the two others we do not know. According to tradition they are Dismas and Gestas.

When the sun arose this particular morning each of them looked with hope for release, for it was customary on the day of the Passover for the governor to release a prisoner to the people. Thus the redemption of Israel from Egypt was commemorated by a captive receiving his freedom.

Pilate knew he would be called upon to pick someone for release. The urgency became acute when Herod returned Our Lord to Pilate, who in turn called together the chief priests, magistrates, and the people and said to them, "You have presented unto me this man as one who perverted the people, and behold I, having examined Him *before* you, find no cause in this man, in those things wherein you accuse Him. No! Nor Herod either. For I sent you to him and behold nothing worthy of death is done unto Him."

Pilate had Christ on his hands. The problem was how to get rid of Him. His imagination leaped to the prison. He had a great idea politically! Morally it was weak, and even rotten. He would allow the people to vote on the prisoner who would be released. Pilate probably was anxious to insure the release of Christ and in order to do so, chose from among those three men one who was called Barabbas.

Barabbas was well known or "notable," and very likely, as his name indicates, the son of a Rabbi (Matthew 27:16). Saint John tells us he was a robber (John 18:40). Later he was arrested for sedition and for a murder committed on that occasion (Luke 23:19).

He was, in our language, a "revolutionist." When it is recalled that Israel was under the Romans, the term "revolutionist" is to be understood as a "patriot" or a member of Israel's underground. He was interested in throwing off the yoke of political tyranny. The whole nation had been palpitating for a deliverer from the Roman yoke. Hence they asked of Christ, "Are you the one who is to come, or should we look for another?" (Matthew 11:3). For two centuries Israel had no Judaeus Macchabeus to lead a revolt against Caesar. Barabbas stepped in to fill this role, and in his enthusiasm for the freedom of his people he had committed a murder; and, what was more serious to Pilate, he was a seditionist.

Pilate sought to confuse the issue by choosing a prisoner who was guilty of exactly the same charge as Christ, namely, sedition against Caesar. In a few minutes, two figures stand before the multitude on the pretentious white marble floor of the Praetorium. Pilate sits on a raised platform, surrounded by the imperial guard. Barabbas, on one side, blinks in the sunlight. He had not seen it in months. On the other side stands Christ.

Here are two men accused of revolution. Barabbas appealed to national grievances; Christ to conscience. Barabbas would release fetters and ignore sin. Our Lord would release man from sin and fetters would cease to be. The trumpets sound. Order is restored. Pilate steps forward and addresses the mob, "Which one do you want me to release to you, Barabbas or Jesus called Messiah?" (Matthew 27:17).

The question of Pilate had all the air of democracy and free election but it was only its cheap facsimile. Ponder his question. Consider first the people to whom it was addressed, then the question itself. The people themselves were not inclined to put Our Lord to death (Matthew 27:20). For that reason some demagogues stirred among the people and persuaded them that they should ask for Barabbas. There is always a ragtag, bobtail group, careless and thoughtless, who are ready to be at the mercy of that kind of oratory which has been called "the harlot of the arts." The people can be misled by false leaders; the very ones who shout "Hosanna!" on Sunday can shout "Crucify!" on Friday.

Herein is revealed the grave danger to democracy, for what happened to those people happens again and again in history: the danger of the people degenerating into *masses*.

What is the difference? By the people we mean persons who make their own decisions, who are governed by their consciences, who are self-determined by moral purpose, and who uphold the right even in the face of demagogy. By the masses we mean the people who have ceased to be governed interiorly by their consciences, who are determined in their thinking by a few irresponsible leaders on the outside, who are susceptible to the mental contagion of propaganda, and who have therefore a psychological readiness for slavery.

What happened on that Good Friday morning was that through propagandists the people became the masses. A democracy with a conscience became a mobocracy with power. When a democracy loses its moral sense, it can vote itself right out of democracy.

When Pilate asked: "Which one do you want me to release to you?" (Matthew 27:17), he was not holding a fair democratic election. He was assuming that a vote means the right to choose between Innocence and Guilt, Evil and Goodness, Right and Wrong.

This is wrong. True democracy never votes on Innocence and Guilt, for both Pilate's court and Herod's court declared Our Lord innocent. Every democracy is rooted in a theological absolute and political and economic relativities. To the eternal glory of American democracy, when we go to the polls we do not vote on whether we shall have a regime of justice or a regime of injustice; we vote rather on relatively good means to a good end. Our democracy assumes that there is an absolute about which we do not vote. There are certain truths that are never challenged, for example, "All men are endowed by their Creator with certain inalienable rights." It is because we never question this and other absolutes that we are free to vote. It is this that makes America great.

De Tocqueville first thought America would never survive because of its conflicting groups, classes, and points of view. But later on he discovered that beneath them all was a common tradition, a common heritage, a common faith, which no one ever challenged.

One of the reasons why European democracies disintegrated is because they did not have the common fund of absolutes. The rugged rationalism of Voltaire, the sentimental humanism of Rousseau, though strong enough to foment mass upheaval, were not strong enough to create a faith. In America, in addition to having a political system, we have a political faith. Because of this our political parties never have been completely partisan. The other party is not exiled. The majority party becomes the custodian of minority rights. Because the parties agree on great ideas they can differ on political questions.

> *Unitas in necessariis*
> *Diversitas in contingentibus*
> *Caritas in omnibus*

In answer to Pilate's question, the masses thundered back, "Release to us Barabbas!" Pilate could hardly believe his ears. Barabbas could hardly believe his ears, either! Was he about to be a free man? For the first time he became aware that he might now carry on his revolt. He turned his swollen burning face toward the Nazarene. He meant to measure his rival from head to foot, but his glance no longer dared to rise. There was something about His eyes which read his soul, as if that Nazarene was really sorry for him because he was free.

"But the whole multitude together cried out, saying, 'Away with this man! Release Barabbas to us'" (Luke 23:18). "Pilate again said to them in reply, 'Then what do you want me to do with the man you call the King of the Jews?'" (Mark 15:12) "still wishing to release Jesus" (Luke 23:20). "But they continued their shouting, saying: 'Crucify him! Crucify him!'" (Luke 23:21).

"And he said to them the third time: 'Why, what evil has this man done? I found him guilty of no capital crime. Therefore I shall have him flogged and then release him.' With loud shouts, however, they persisted in calling for his crucifixion, and their voices prevailed" (Luke 23:22,23). "The verdict of Pilate was that their demand should be granted. So he released the man who had been imprisoned for rebellion and murder, for whom they asked, and he handed Jesus over to them to deal with as they wished" (Luke 23:24,25).

The majority is not always right. Majority is right in the field of the relative, but not in the absolute. Majority is a legitimate test, so long as voting is based on conscience and not on propaganda. Truth does not win when numbers *qua* numbers become decisive. Numbers alone can decide a beauty queen but not Justice. Beauty is a matter of taste, but Justice is tasteless. Right is still right if nobody is right, and wrong is still wrong if everybody is wrong. The first poll in the history of Christianity was wrong!

Barabbas was amazed at a favor beyond his fondest hopes. He had fought for political liberty. He had procured the names of a few quislings, had sabotaged Roman works, had organized a few patriotic followers, had gained some prestige by being arrested, for arrest heightens the prestige of revolutionists. But all that was nothing compared to the deafening shouts for him as their leader, their hero. He was no longer an outlaw, but a free man. It meant death for Christ—but that was *nothing!*

Barabbas was free! He had four freedoms:

1. Freedom from fear—no more Roman prisons.
2. Freedom from want—no more coarse bread and water.
3. Freedom of speech—he could once more talk revolution.
4. Freedom of religion—he could talk against religion if he wanted to.

Freedom for him meant freedom from something. And it was an empty freedom. It was as colorless as water when he thought it would be red like wine. He noticed that after the voting no one followed him. It was the queerest election in the history of the world; no torchlight procession for the victor, no one hoisted him on shoulders, no mob followed the victor with cheers. But everyone followed the defeated candidate. To have the mob with him he had to follow the mob that followed Christ. With them, unnoticed, he moved down to the basement of Pilate's fortress where he watched the scourging of the defeated candidate.

When the scourging was done, Barabbas followed the defeated candidate up the hill of Calvary—it was still the only way Barabbas could have a following. Barabbas noticed that his two fellow prisoners were also there. They were not so fortunate as to have been nominated for election. They were to be crucified on either side of Our Lord, Dismas on His right, and Gestas on His left.

When finally all the three crosses were unfurled against the dark sky, Barabbas heard Gestas on His left curse, swear, and ask to be taken down. But he also heard Dismas on His right ask to be taken up: "Remember me when you come into your kingdom" (Luke 23:42). To which plea came back the divine promise: "This day you shall be with me in Paradise" (Luke 23:43).

What kind of freedom was this with which Dismas was satisfied? Can one be nailed to a cross and still be free? Can He Who is pinned to that central tree be the giver of freedom, the guardian and savior of liberty? Then Barabbas saw that the freedom for which he was seeking was not the freedom to be free *from* something, but that the only true freedom is to be free *for* something. Now he sees freedom as not an end, but a means. Freedom is for the sake of doing something worth doing.

1. What good is freedom from fear unless there is someone to love?
2. What good is freedom from want unless there is a Justice to be served?
3. What good is freedom of speech unless there is a Truth to defend?
4. What good is freedom of religion unless there is a God to worship?

Barabbas now would have given anything to have been Dismas. Dismas was free! He was not. Only nailed love is free; unnailed love can compel and therefore destroy freedom. Hearken, revolutionists!

Follow not Barabbas, the revolutionist who would re-make society to remake man; but rather Christ, the Revo-lutionist Who would remake man in order to remake society.

Believe in violence, yes, but not the violence that draws a sword against a neighbor, a class or race or color, but rather draws it against self, to cut out lust, envy, greed, and hate. Attend ye, believers in violence! Be violent not against fellowman but against selfishness, for "the kingdom of heaven suffers violence, and the violent are taking it by force" (Matthew 11:12).

Learn, all who prattle about freedom in a land of freedom, that *the only true freedom in the world is the freedom to be a saint!*

❁

In the deserts of the heart
Let the healing fountain start.
In the prison of his days
Teach the free man how to praise.
—W.H. AUDEN

CHAPTER SEVEN

❀

The Scars of Christ: A Lesson on Enduring Faith

The world following a war wears its scars. Often millions of displaced persons wander haggard, haunted, and hunted across the vast expanses of the world, and as they fall, the very earth that should have ministered to them takes the measure of their unmade graves. Calloused hands, weary from a cross of forced labor, look up in vain for Cyreneans to lift their burden; wounded soldiers limp across a world they fought to make free, and yet see not that freedom for which their dead comrades went to graves as to their beds.

While our earth wears these scars, who can bring us

hope that better days lie ahead, and that all this pain and anguish is not a mockery and a snare?

One thing is certain: No healing can come to our broken wings from that liberal Christ invented by the nineteenth century, who made Him only a moral teacher like Socrates and Mohammed or Confucius, and bound like them in the fetters of death.

The only one who can bring solace to our times is a Christ with scars, Who Himself had passed through death to give us hope and life, and this is the Christ of Easter morn. What figure large in the Easter story are the scars of Christ. Magdalen, who was always at His feet, either in Simon's house or at the cross, is there again in the garden; and not until she sees on those feet the red livid memories of Calvary's war does she recognize her Lord and cry out, "Rabboni!"—Master.

Then Christ came to the skeptical, doubting world in the person of Thomas, whose melancholy made him a doubter. When told by the other disciples that they had seen the Lord, Thomas said to them, "Unless I see the mark of the nails in his hands, unless I put my finger into the place where the nails were, and my hands into his side, I will not believe it" (John 20:25).

Eight days later when the disciples were in the room and Thomas with them, "Jesus came, although the doors were locked, and stood in their midst and said, 'Peace be with you.' Then He said to Thomas, 'Put your finger here and see my hands, and bring your hand and put it into my side, and do not be unbelieving, but believe.' Thomas answered and said to him, 'My Lord, and my God!'" (John 20:26-28).

The kind of Christ the world needs today is the Virile Christ, who can unfurl to an evil world the pledge of victory in His own Body, offered in bloody sacrifice for salvation. No false gods who are immune from pain and sorrow can solace us in these tragic days.

Take out of our lives the Christ of the Scars, Who is the Son of the Living God, Who rose from the dead by the power of God, and what assurance have we that evil shall not triumph over good? If He Who came to this earth to teach the dignity of the human soul, Who could challenge a sinful world to convict Him of sin, had no other issue and destiny than to hang on a common tree with common criminals and thieves to make a Roman holiday, then each of us may say, "If this is what happens to a good man, then why should I lead a good life?" What motivation is there for virtue if the greatest of all injustices can go unredressed, and the noblest of all lives can go unvindicated?

What am I to think of a God Who would look down unmoved on this spectacle of Innocence going to the gallows and would not pull out the nails and put a scepter there; or would not even send an angel to snatch a crown of thorns and place a garland there?

What am I to think of human nature if this white flower of blameless life is trampled under the hobnailed boots of Roman executioners and then is destined to rot in the earth like all crushed flowers rot? Would it not send forth the greater stench because of its primal sweetness and make us hate not only the God Who had no care for truth and love, but even our fellowman for being party to His death? If this is the end of goodness, then why be good at all? If this is what happens to justice, then let anarchy reign.

But if He is not only man but God; if He is not a teacher of humanitarian ethics, but a Redeemer; if He can take the worst this world has to offer and then by the power of God rise above it; if He, the unarmed, can make war with no other weapon than goodness and pardon, so that slain has the gain, and they who kill the foe lose the day, then who shall be without hope as the Risen Christ shows us His Hands and Side?

What do the scars of Christ teach us? They teach us that life is a struggle: that our condition of a final resurrection is exactly the same as His; that unless there is a cross in our lives, there will never be an empty tomb; unless there is a Good Friday, there will never be an Easter Sunday; unless there is a crown of thorns, there will never be the halo of light; and unless we suffer with Him, we shall not rise with Him.

The Christ of the Scars gave us no peace which banishes strife, for God hates peace in those that are destined for war against evil.

The scars are not only reminders that life is warfare,

but they are also pledges of victory in that war. Our Blessed Lord said, "I have overcome the world." By this He means that He has overcome evil in principle. The victory is assured, only the good news has not yet leaked out. Evil will never be able to be stronger than it was on that particular day, for the worst thing that evil can do is not to ruin cities and to wage wars and to drop atomic bombs against the good and the living. The worst thing that evil can do is to kill God. Having been defeated in that, in its strongest moment, when evil wore its greatest armor, it can never be victorious again.

Think not, then, that the Jesus of the Scars and His victory over evil give us immunity from evil and woe, pain and sorrow, crucifixion and death. What He offers is not immunity from evil in the physical world, but a chance for forgiveness for sin in our souls. The final conquest of physical evil will come in the resurrection of the just. But He does teach a noble army of the world's sufferers to bear the worst this life has to offer with courage and serenity, to regard all of its trials as "the shade of His hand outstretched caressingly," and to transfigure some of life's greatest pains into the richest gains of the spiritual life.

With Saint Paul, then, we cry out in an ecstasy of triumph, "What will separate us from the love of Christ? Will anguish, or distress, or persecution, or famine, or nakedness, or peril, or the sword? …No, in all these things we conquer overwhelmingly through Him who loved us.

For I am convinced that neither death, nor life, nor angels, nor principalities, nor powers, nor things to come, nor might, nor height, nor depth, nor any other creature shall be able to separate us from the love of God, which is in Christ Jesus Our Lord" (Romans 8:35–39).

Over against the Christian faith in the Risen Christ is a materialist philosophy that puts its faith not in God but in man, and principally one man who fulfills the role of the dictator.

Our Western world sees the danger in this new faith but is impotent to oppose it, for its defenses rest only on the vacillating and fluctuating opinion of politicians and leaders who have no convincing standards to offer the people, who themselves are without a faith and, therefore, can never give a faith. What has made the cause of the Western world weaker is its aversion to doctrine, its hatred of dogma, which leaves it without an ideology to oppose an ideology—and therefore powerless to deal with the enemy, except by offering a few indifferent cabinet changes.

Because our Western world has turned its back upon those authentic fires that were lighted at the eternal altars of the Living God, it leaves the people's torches unlit. Now like a moth in the dark, the Western man flutters to a smoky candle of totalitarianism, flies into it, and is lost. The struggle today is too unequal. The materialistic forces of the world have a philosophy of life; the West has none.

Since basically all quarrels are theological, it follows that if we surrender the faith in Christ that made our Western Christian civilization, then we can offer no goals to journeys and no hope to a lost generation. You cannot oppose an ideology with an opinion, or a philosophy of life with appeasing compromises. The mere fact that you give your right arm to a bear is no guarantee that he will not take your left.

The real case against the new materialism must be a theological one. Doctrine must be invoked to combat doctrine. This is certain. Unless we can give people of the Western world a faith to combat the false faith, the fanatical disciples of world revolution will capture and inflame the loyalty of millions, and we shall be destroyed by what is false within.

If, however, we have faith that in the conflict between good and evil God still works in history, then ultimate victory of good can come out of tragedy, as once more eternal love becomes triumphant when sin has done its worst.

If it would seem that the scars of Christ are but small and feeble security against the well-armed powers of evil, then look back to the former conflict between the forces of good and evil in the persons of David and Goliath. Goliath assumed that any champion who would come forth to meet him must himself be a spearman, quite forgetful that the cause of God rests on other arms than those of spears.

David took a slingshot, a rather harmless-looking instrument hewn from the forest, and choosing five small stones from a brook he went out to meet the Philistine.

So hard-set was Goliath's mind that it was to be a battle of armaments that when he saw David coming to him with no armor on his body and nothing in his hand except five tiny stones and a sling, he took umbrage at the insult and said to David, "Am I a dog, that you come to me with a staff?" (1 Samuel 17:43). And David answered and said, "You come to me with a sword, and with a spear, and with a shield: but I come to you in the name of the Lord of hosts, the God of the armies of Israel, which you have defied" (1 Samuel 17:45).

Goliath stepped forward panoplied from head to foot and with only his unvisored forehead as a target. With the first shot from his sling, David struck Goliath on the head, the stone being fixed in his forehead as he fell to the earth. Having no other sword than that of the Philistine, David took it and cut off his head.

One day this prefigurement was realized when Christ on Good Friday came to do battle with the Goliath of evil that was supported by the power of all the governments in the world. Taking no other armor than a cross from the forest, which looked like the slingshot of David, He picked up from the cascading brooks of the world's hate not five stones, but five scars, any one of which would have been enough to have redeemed the world, and with them slew the Goliath of evil.

If He, our leader, wore five scars, then must we His soldiers be prepared on the day of the Great Review when he comes to judge the living and the dead, to show Him the scars we won in His cause and in His Name. To each of us He will say, "Show Me your hands and your side." Woe, then, to us who come down Calvary with hands unscarred and white!

If there is any one of those five scars that we would choose as David chose one of the stones to slay the Goliath of evil, it would be the scar that was made by the sergeant of the Roman army, when he ran a lance in the side of the Savior. Until the day of the final victory, we shall march confidently under the great Captain Who wears for the first time in history the decoration that humanity pinned on His Breast: the Purple Heart of the All-Loving God!

❀

O come, let us sing to the Lord:
let us heartily rejoice in the strength
of our salvation.
—PRAYER BOOK 95:1

About the Author

FULTON J. SHEEN (1895–1979) was one of the best-loved prelates of twentieth-century Catholicism. A prolific writer and orator, a distinguished scholar and teacher, an influential master of the media, Sheen was one of the most effective communicators of our time. His scores of books have offered inspiration, profound thought, and penetrating analyses of Christian faith and life.